Jacqueline Kennedy
CULTURAL ICON

BY ANNETTE GULATI

The Child's World®
childsworld.com

Published by The Child's World®
1980 Lookout Drive • Mankato, MN 56003-1705
800-599-READ • www.childsworld.com

Photographs ©: Bettmann/Getty Images, cover, 1; AP Images, 5, 6; Cecil Yates/AP Images, 8; Dalmas/Sipa Press/AP Images, 10; Owen/Black Star/Newscom, 12; Arnie Sachs/dpa/picture-alliance/Newscom, 14; Cecil Stoughton/White House Photographs/John F. Kennedy Presidential Library and Museum/Boston, 17; Eddie Adams/AP Images, 19

ISBN 9781503823990
LCCN 2017944740

Printed in the United States of America
PA02362

JB
ONASSIS
JACQUELINE

ABOUT THE AUTHOR

Annette Gulati is the author of four nonfiction books for children. She also writes stories, articles, poems, crafts, and activities for magazines and educational publishers. She lives in Seattle, Washington, with her family.

TABLE OF CONTENTS

FAST FACTS

Full Name

- Jacqueline (Jackie) Bouvier Kennedy Onassis

Birthdate

- July 28, 1929, in Southampton, New York

Husband

- President John Fitzgerald Kennedy

Children

- Caroline and John Jr.

Years in White House

- 1961–1963

Accomplishments

- Completed the **restoration** of the White House.
- Served as a goodwill **ambassador** while traveling around the world.
- Supported American arts and **culture**. She invited artists, writers, musicians, and scientists to the White House.

5

Chapter 1

RESTORATION OF THE WHITE HOUSE

Jacqueline (Jackie) Kennedy stood before a television camera in the White House. She brushed her hands over her red suit and adjusted the string of pearls around her neck. Then she folded her hands and began speaking softly to the reporter. At first, Jackie found it strange talking while a dark camera captured her every move. But as she continued, she grew more excited to explain the restoration project she had completed at the White House. She led the reporter and camera crew into the Diplomatic Reception Room and pointed out wallpaper created in 1834. They moved to another room.

◄ Jackie Kennedy gave reporter Charles Collingwood a tour of the White House in 1962.

▲ Jackie and John got married on September 12, 1953.

Jackie told the reporter about a fireplace mantel from 1817.

When her husband John became president, Jackie wanted her new home, the White House, to be beautiful. She thought it should show America's history.

So the First Lady and her team of experts searched for **antique** furniture and artwork. They found some that had belonged to past presidents. "Everything in the White House must have a reason for being there," she said.[1] At the end of the tour, Jackie smiled. Millions of Americans watched the program. She even won an Emmy award for her role. The award acknowledges outstanding television.

Jackie grew up in New York City. She did well in school and was known for being clever and artistic.

When she was 11 years old, Jackie visited the White House with her mother. But she was disappointed. "All I remember is shuffling through," she said.[2] She wanted to buy a pamphlet so she could learn more about the house's history. But no such thing existed. So when Jackie became First Lady, she helped create a White House guide booklet for all visitors.

Chapter 2

A POPULAR FIRST LADY

Thousands of French citizens lined the streets of Paris, France. They waved American flags and shouted "Jackie!" as the First Lady passed.[3] She smiled and waved back. It was May 1961. Jackie had only been the First Lady for a few months, and she was happy to be in Paris with John. Her eyes swept across the city, noting familiar buildings and landmarks. Jackie had studied there for a year during college, and she was excited to return.

At a dinner the next evening, Jackie wore a long dress decorated with flowers. She sat next to the French president, Charles de Gaulle.

◄ John and Jackie met with French president Charles de Gaulle (right) and his wife, Yvonne (second from right), during their trips to France.

▲ Jackie and her children, Caroline and John Jr.

Jackie **translated** as de Gaulle and John spoke to each other, and de Gaulle was impressed by the First Lady. John later said, "I am the man who accompanied Jacqueline Kennedy to Paris."[4]

People flocked to see the First Lady wherever she went. World leaders thought she was energetic and pleasant. Jackie impressed everyone with her intelligence. She was **fluent** in three languages. On a trip with the president to Venezuela, the First Lady gave a speech in Spanish. Jackie realized she had a lot of influence on people. Still, she missed her two children when she was traveling.

The world was also interested in the First Lady's clothing. Jackie had her own fashion designer. She wore elegant dresses and suits. She made pillbox hats popular. Photos of her fashions showed up in magazines and newspapers. Women around the world wanted to dress like her.

> "I'll be a wife and mother first, then First Lady."[5]
>
> —*Jackie Kennedy*

Chapter 3

PROMOTING ARTS AND CULTURE

On May 11, 1962, Jackie put on a long pink dress and white gloves. She was hosting a special dinner for the French minister of culture, André Malraux. The White House soon filled with musicians, artists, and writers. Everyone sat down to a delicious meal of lobster and cream puffs. Then they listened as three musicians took the stage and filled the room with music.

Malraux was delighted. He leaned over to whisper in Jackie's ear. He wanted to send France's most famous painting to the United States for its citizens to enjoy.

One year later, millions of Americans flocked to museums in Washington, DC, and New York City.

◀ Jackie and André Malraux attended the *Mona Lisa* exhibit on January 8, 1963.

They wanted to catch a glimpse of the *Mona Lisa*. Jackie was very happy. "I hoped his visit would call attention to the importance of the arts," she said.[6]

Before she married John, Jackie had worked as a photographer and writer. For her job, Jackie would wander through the streets, snapping pictures and interviewing the public. She believed the arts were important. Her husband did, too. So the Kennedys continued to host many dinners that promoted the arts.

The First Lady had a stage built in the White House where famous dancers, actors, and musicians performed. But she also found artists who were not yet well known and invited them to the White House. The Kennedys celebrated American artists of all kinds.

Jackie traveled around the world as First Lady. ▶
In 1962 she visited India.

Chapter 4

MOVING ON

A dazed Jackie was guided into the president's airplane in Dallas, Texas, on November 22, 1963. There was a sense of panic in the air. People rushed on and off the parked airplane, preparing for an unplanned ceremony to appoint a new president. John F. Kennedy had just been **assassinated**. Jackie stood silently in a pink suit splattered in blood. Vice President Lyndon B. Johnson stood next to her. Jackie listened as Johnson was sworn in as the next president of the United States.

A few days later, in Washington, DC, Jackie bravely walked down the street with John's casket. She wore a black dress and veil. She held back her tears.

◀ Jackie modeled John's funeral after President Abraham Lincoln's funeral procession.

Afterward, Jackie packed up her things and moved to New York with her children, Caroline and John Jr. She wanted privacy. She also wanted to focus on being a good mother.

Five years later, Jackie married again and moved to Greece. However, she returned to New York after her second husband died in 1975. She followed her passion for reading and writing and became an editor for a book publisher. Throughout this time, she never forgot John. Jackie wanted people to remember him, so she chose an **architect** to plan the John F. Kennedy Presidential Library and Museum. She wanted the building to be a work of art and to honor John's memory. She helped choose pictures, books, and personal objects for display. The library and museum opened in 1979.

> "I always wanted to be some kind of writer."[7]
>
> —*Jackie Kennedy*

Jackie also spent time with her children and grandchildren. Before she died in 1994, she worked hard to promote literature, art, and American history. Her influence on the White House is still seen by visitors today.

THINK ABOUT IT

- Jackie worked hard to advance arts and culture in the United States. Why do you think she was interested in doing this? What benefits could Americans gain by experiencing arts and culture?
- Jackie wanted to restore the White House. Why do you think this was important to her?
- Because of John's sudden death, Jackie's role as First Lady came to an abrupt end and her life changed drastically. How do you think this experience impacted her?

GLOSSARY

ambassador (am-BAS-ud-ur): An ambassador is a special representative of a country. Jackie was a goodwill ambassador of the United States.

antique (an-TEEK): An object is antique if it is made at an earlier time in history. The White House is filled with antique furniture and artwork.

architect (AR-ki-tekt): An architect is a person who designs buildings. Jackie hired an architect to design the John F. Kennedy Presidential Library.

assassinated (uh-SAS-uh-nate-ed): To be assassinated is to be suddenly murdered by someone. President John F. Kennedy was assassinated.

culture (KUL-chur): Culture is the customs and arts of a group of people. Jackie was interested in French culture.

fluent (FLOO-uhnt): To be fluent in a language is to have the ability to use the language easily and accurately. Jackie was fluent in three languages.

restoration (reh-stor-RAY-shun): A restoration is the return of something to its original condition. Jackie completed a White House restoration.

translated (trans-LATE-ed): Words are translated when their meaning is explained in a different language. Jackie translated French into English so her husband could understand the French president, Charles de Gaulle.

SOURCE NOTES

1. "The White House Restoration." *John F. Kennedy Presidential Library and Museum.* John F. Kennedy Presidential Library and Museum, n.d. Web. 26 June 2017.

2. Ibid.

3. Clint Hill. *Mrs. Kennedy and Me.* New York, NY: Gallery Books, 2012. Print. 69.

4. Ibid. 70–72.

5. Bill Adler, ed. *The Eloquent Jacqueline Kennedy Onassis.* New York, NY: William Morrow, 2004. Print. 4.

6. Carl Sferrazza Anthony. *As We Remember Her.* New York, NY: HarperCollins, 1997. Print. 168.

7. Bill Adler, ed. *The Eloquent Jacqueline Kennedy Onassis.* New York, NY: William Morrow, 2004. Print. 20.

TO LEARN MORE

Books

Bader, Bonnie. *Who Was Jacqueline Kennedy?* New York, NY: Grosset & Dunlap, 2016.

Krull, Kathleen. *A Kids' Guide to America's First Ladies.* New York, NY: HarperCollins, 2017.

Wing, Natasha. *When Jackie Saved Grand Central.* Boston, MA: Houghton Mifflin Harcourt, 2017.

Web Sites

Visit our Web site for links about Jacqueline Kennedy:

childsworld.com/links

Note to Parents, Teachers, and Librarians: We routinely verify our Web links to make sure they are safe and active sites. So encourage your readers to check them out!

INDEX